READING POWER

19th Century American Inventors

The Inventions of

Granville Woods

The Railroad Telegraph System
and the "Third Rail"

Holly Cefrey

The Rosen Publishing Group's
PowerKids Press™
New York

Published in 2003 by The Rosen Publishing Group, Inc.
29 East 21st Street, New York, NY 10010

First Edition

Book Design: Daniel Hosek

Photo Credits: Cover, p. 20 © AP/Wide World Photos; pp. 4–5 © Corbis; pp. 5 (inset), 10–11, 15, 16 Culver Pictures; pp. 6–7, 13 © Bettmann/ Corbis; pp. 9, 10 (inset), 17, 19 United States Patent and Trademark Office; p. 14 © Science, Industry and Business Library, The New York Public Library, Astor, Lenox and Tilden Foundations; p. 21 © Robert Landau/Corbis

Library of Congress Cataloging-in-Publication Data

Cefrey, Holly.
The inventions of Granville Woods : the railroad telegraph system and the "third rail" / Holly Cefrey.
    p. cm. — (19th century American inventors)
Summary: Provides a biographical sketch of Granville Woods, sometimes known as the "Black Edison," and descriptions of some of his inventions.
ISBN 0-8239-6442-6 (library binding)
1. Woods, Granville, 1856-1910—Juvenile literature. 2. Telegraphers—Biography—Juvenile literature. 3. Railroads—Telegraph—History—Juvenile literature. [1. Woods, Granville, 1856-1910. 2. Telegraphers. 3. Inventors. 4. African Americans—Biography.] I. Title. II. Series.
TK5243.K84 C44 2003
621.3'092—dc21

                                        2002000177

Contents

Young Granville Woods

Granville Woods was born in Columbus, Ohio, on April 23, 1856. His parents were Martha and Tailer Woods. Woods only went to school until he was ten years old. Then he had to go to work to earn money.

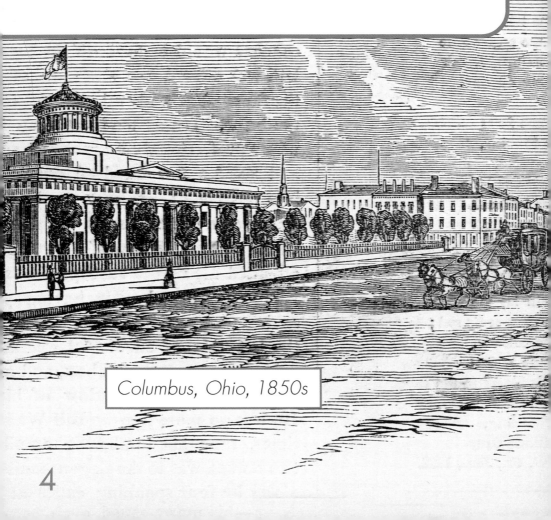

Columbus, Ohio, 1850s

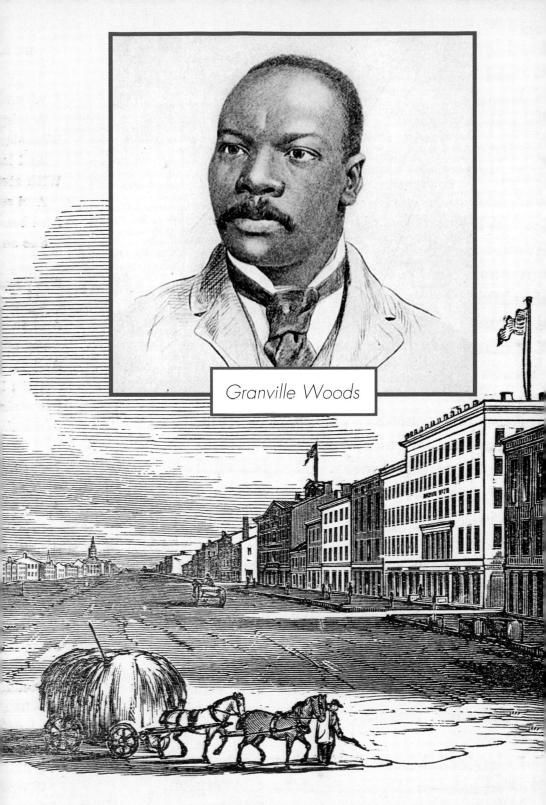

Granville Woods

Learning and Working

Woods's first job was at the age of ten in a machine shop where he learned about trains. At this time, he also read many books and learned about electricity on his own.

New York City, 1870s

At sixteen, he moved to Missouri to work on the Iron Mountain Railroad.

Woods also worked in Illinois and New York City. In New York City, he went to school at night to learn more about electricity.

Going into Business

Around 1880, Woods opened a machine shop in Cincinnati, Ohio. In 1884, he made his first invention, a steam boiler furnace. It made steam engines work better.

(No Model.)

G. T. WOODS.

STEAM BOILER FURNACE.

No. 299,894.   Patented June 3, 1884.

Fig. 1.

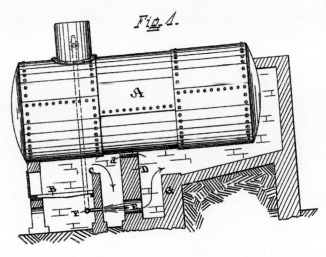

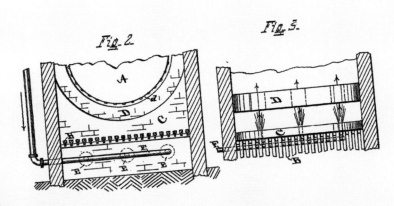

Fig. 2.   Fig. 3.

Inventor
Granville T. Woods
by *L. H. Stone* Atty.

Attest
Carl Spangel.
H. Hamilton

Patent drawing for steam boiler furnace

9

Inventions

In 1887, Woods made one of his most important inventions. It was a telegraph system that made traveling by train safer.

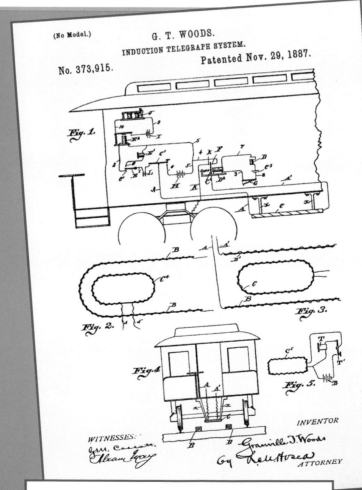

Patent drawing for telegraph system

His invention let train crews find out if there were other trains in front or behind them. Workers at train stations also used the system to keep track of trains in the area.

Before Woods's invention, there were many train crashes.

The famous inventor Thomas Edison was working on an idea that was like Woods's telegraph system. Edison took Woods to court and said that Woods had used his idea. Edison lost his case.

However, Edison liked the work that Woods was doing. Edison offered him a job, but Woods turned Edison down. Woods liked working on his own.

The Fact Box

Woods sold the patents for most of his inventions to other companies.

Thomas Edison

Woods also invented the "third rail" system for trains. The third rail system gives trains more electricity to use. Today, Woods's third rail system is still being used by many subway trains.

Trains and trolleys, or electric streetcars, had a special part that attached to the third rail.

Many subways, like this one in New York City, started to use the third rail soon after it was invented.

Third rail

Woods continued to help make travel by train better. Starting in 1902, he made inventions that improved train brakes. The inventions allowed trains to stop more quickly and safely. Woods also improved the trolley system.

Woods's inventions helped make the trolley system better.

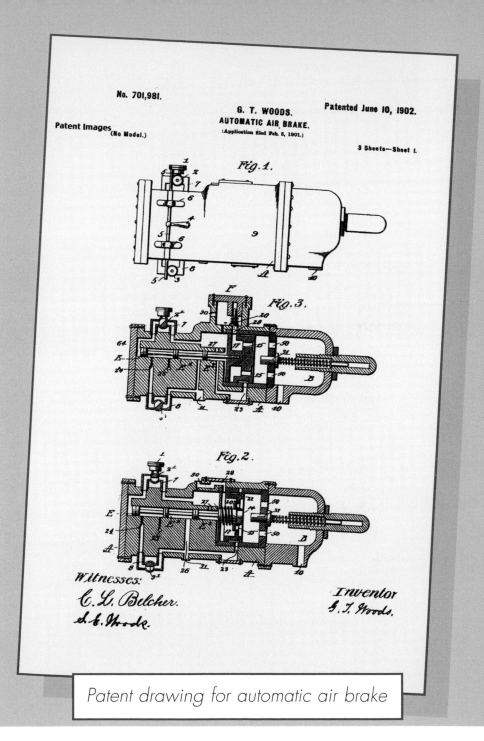

Patent drawing for automatic air brake

Woods also invented an incubator, which made it possible to heat 50,000 chicken eggs at a time. An incubator helps eggs to hatch. A form of Woods's invention is still being used today.

"Mr. Woods, who is the greatest electrician in the world, still continues to add to his long list of electrical inventions."

Catholic Tribune
Cincinnati, Ohio
April 1, 1887

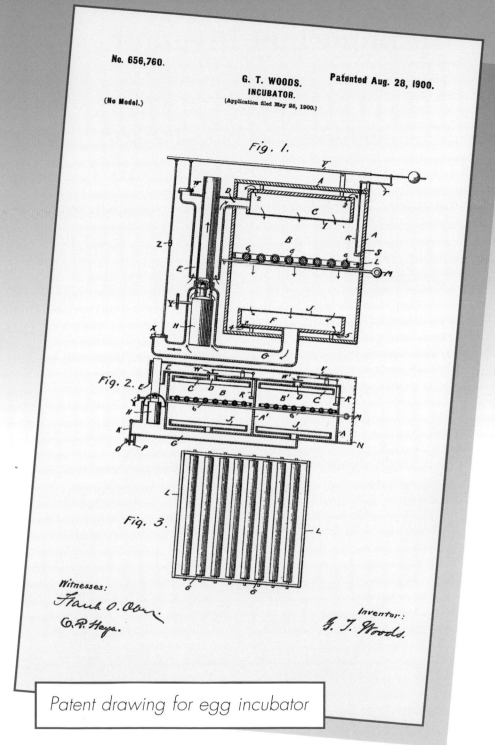

Patent drawing for egg incubator

An Important Inventor

Granville Woods died on January 30, 1910, in New York City. He had more than 60 patents for his inventions. About 50 of his inventions were used by the railroads. Woods's inventions changed the ways that people traveled by making train travel safer and faster. Woods was an important American inventor.

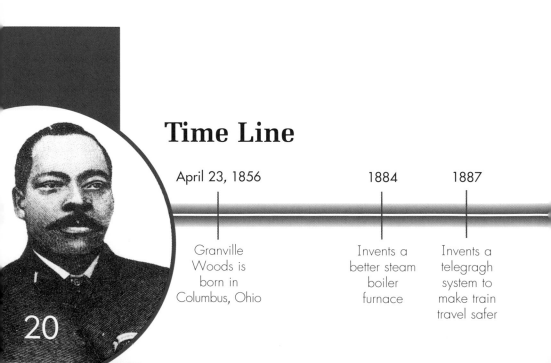

Time Line

April 23, 1856	1884	1887
Granville Woods is born in Columbus, Ohio	Invents a better steam boiler furnace	Invents a telegragh system to make train travel safer

Today, most trains still use Woods's inventions.

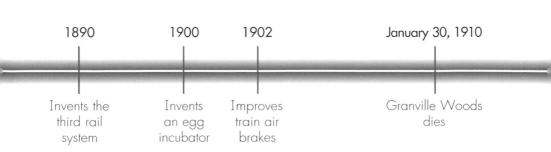

1890	1900	1902	January 30, 1910
Invents the third rail system	Invents an egg incubator	Improves train air brakes	Granville Woods dies

Glossary

electricity (ih-lehk-**trihs**-uh-tee) a form of energy that is used to make light, heat, or motion

furnace (**fehr**-nihs) an enclosed space in which fuel is burned to produce heat

incubator (**ing**-kyuh-bay-tuhr) a machine that keeps eggs warm until they hatch

invention (ihn-**vehn**-shuhn) something new that someone thinks of or makes

inventor (ihn-**vehn**-tor) a person who thinks of or makes something new

patents (**pat**-ehnts) legal papers that give an inventor the right to make or sell his or her invention

telegraph (**tehl**-uh-graf) a machine that sends messages long distances over wires

trolley (**trahl**-ee) an electric streetcar that runs on rails in the streets and carries people

Resources

Books

Five Notable Inventors
by Wade Hudson
Scholastic Incorporated (1995)

African-American Inventors
by Patricia C. McKissack and
Fredrick L. McKissack
Millbrook Press (1994)

Web Sites

Due to the changing nature of Internet links, PowerKids Press has developed an online list of Web sites related to the subjects of this book. This site is updated regularly. Please use this link to access the list:

http://www.powerkidslinks.com/ncai/igw/

Index

Word Count: 411

Note to Librarians, Teachers, and Parents
   If reading is a challenge, Reading Power is a solution! Reading Power is perfect for readers who want high-interest subject matter at an accessible reading level. These fact-filled, photo-illustrated books are designed for readers who want straightforward vocabulary, engaging topics, and a manageable reading experience. With clear picture/text correspondence, leveled Reading Power books put the reader in charge. Now readers have the power to get the information they want and the skills they need in a user-friendly format.